Design
Elements 2

Design
Elements 2

A Visual Reference by
Richard Hora
Mies Hora

The Art Direction Book Company, New York

Dedicated to Fran
and to all those who utilize this book.

Book design by Richard and Mies Hora
Special thanks to
Lee Vitale and W. Thomas Overgard
for their generous assistance.

Art Direction Book Company
10 East 39th Street
New York, New York 10016

Library of Congress Catalog Card Number 81–66127
International Standard Book Number 0-910158–73–8

Forward

The design elements in this collection are
all arranged for your convenience. The
material was selected from a wide variety of
sources, both old and new, with many
created specifically for this volume. It is
organized into specific categories to
speed search-and-find. Each design element
was carefully selected for quality and
general usefulness. All are generously sized
for reproduction purposes. This book
represents over forty years of collection
and use, beginning as a working tool
and eventually developing into a labor of
love. We hope you find *Design Elements 2*
to be the inspirational and easy-to-use
source file that we intended.

Richard Hora
Mies Hora

Introduction

Visual symbols are among the oldest permanent means of communication, dating back some 30,000 years to the caves of Lascaux and Altamira. Our ancestors included the shapes of arrows, hands, and geometric forms in their representations of bulls, horses and mammoths. Clearly those images fulfill some architypal human need. Despite the distances we have travelled from those caves, we find that these same forms remain a compelling means for transmitting information. They are, today as then, an indispensable part of our visual language. In recent years we have seen this tradition enriched by the signs of modern life—television screens, filmstrips, scientific nomenclature, etc.

The availability of a resource in which the very best of these images have been selected and exquisitely rendered for the purposes of reproduction is a great service to all of us, but it is most important to designers. The painstaking care with which Richard and Mies Hora have undertaken this task is reflected in this series of books, which represent an enormous research effort as well as the exercise of astute judgement, taste and skill. Here is a very high level of visual quality and design utility. The thoughtfulness and comprehensive nature of their work makes this series invaluable for the concerned designer.

David C. Levy, Ph.D.
Executive Dean
Parsons School of Design

Reprinted from Design Elements 1

Contents

Forward
Introduction

Arrows 10
Hand Pointers 28

Seals 38
Labels 40
Postage Motifs 56
Tags 58
Blurbs 60
Bursts 62
Banners 64

Hearts 78
Playing Card Symbols 82
Lips 83
Leaf Shapes 84
Trees 90
Crowns/Coronets 94
Flame Shapes 98
Clouds 100
Teardrops 101
Light Bulb Shapes 102
Eggs 103
Pear Shapes, etc. 104
Bell Shapes 106

General
Design Elements
including:
Film Strips 110
Arches/Parabolas 112
Boomerangs 113
Magnets 113
Diamond Shapes 114
Pentagons 114
Springs/Coils 115
Cross Shapes 116
Yin Yang Symbols 122
Atomic Symbols 123
Keyholes 124
Palettes 124
Hour Glasses 124
Infinity Symbols 125
Dart Boards 126
Globes 127

Arrows
Hand Pointers

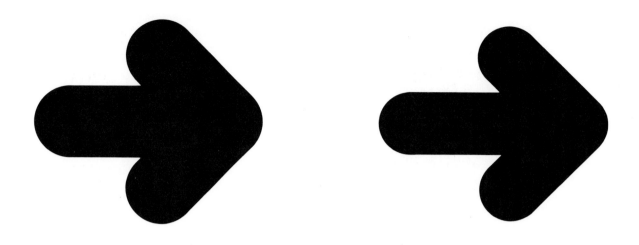

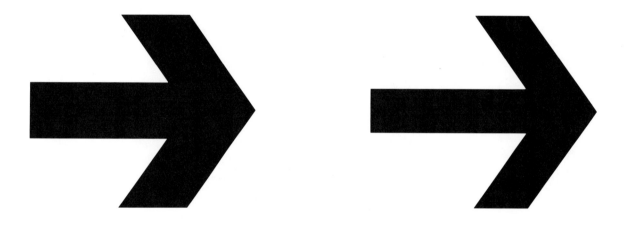

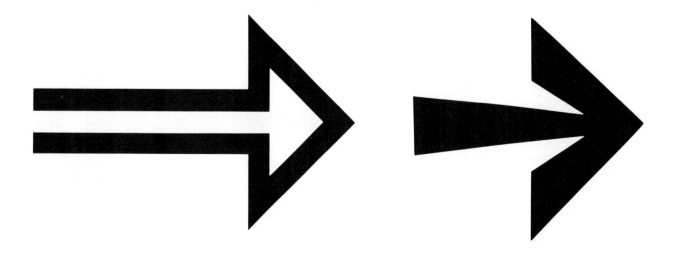

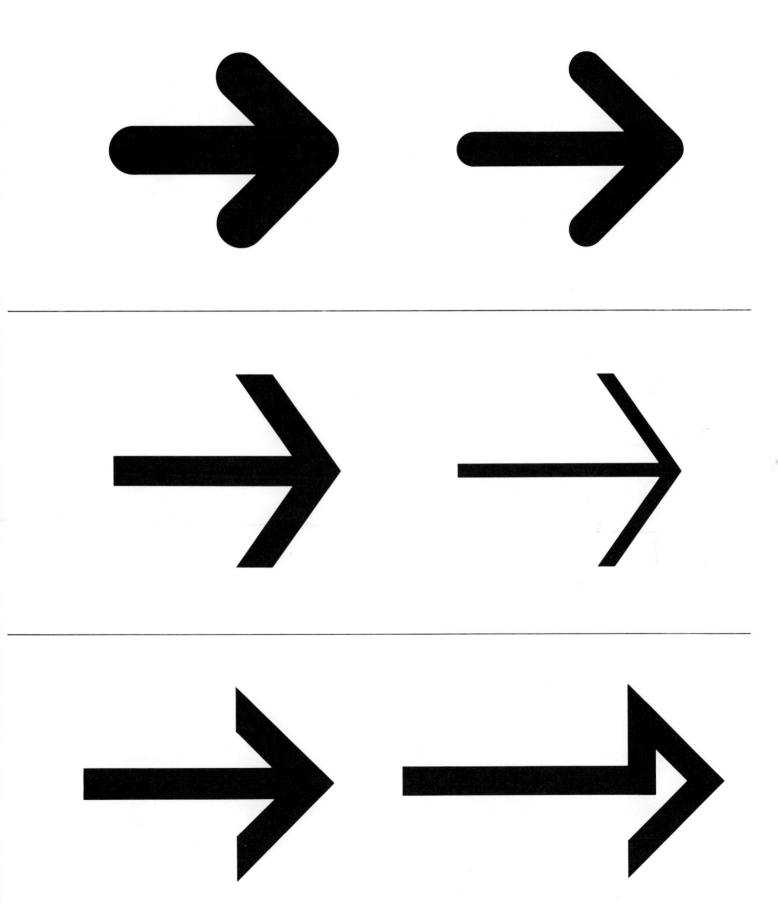

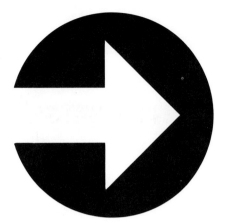

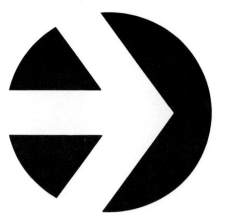

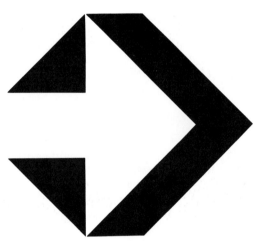

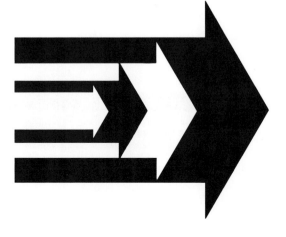

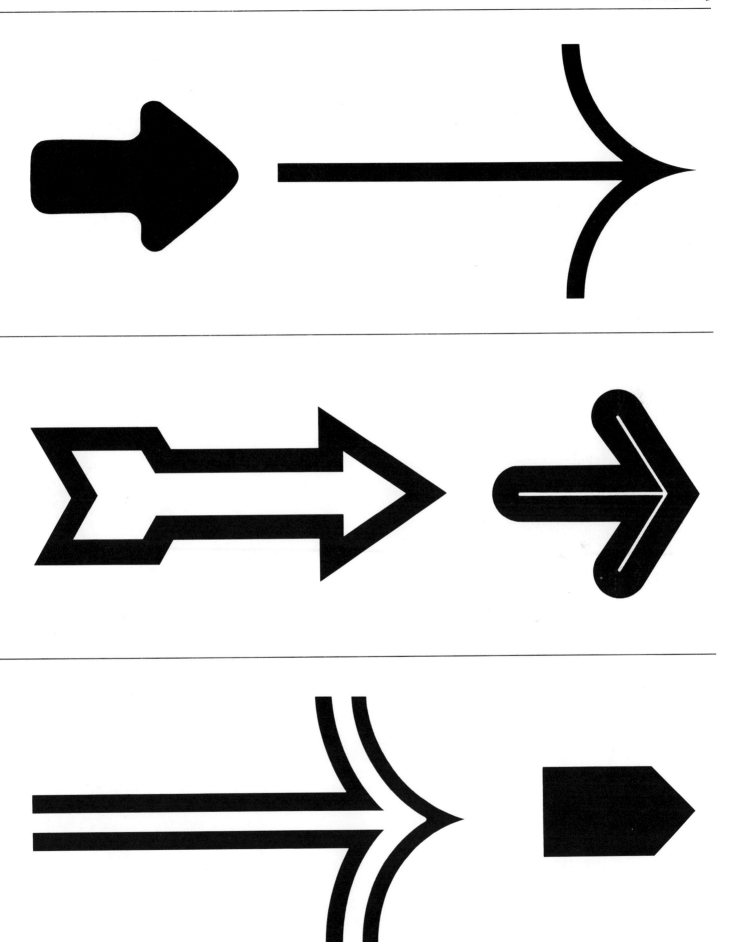

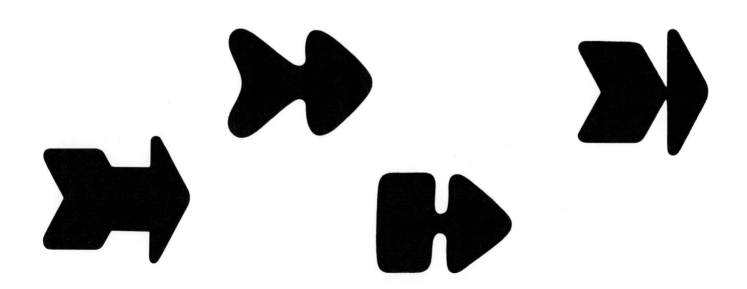

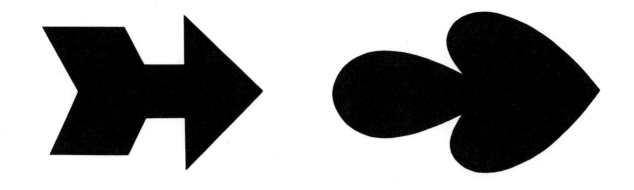

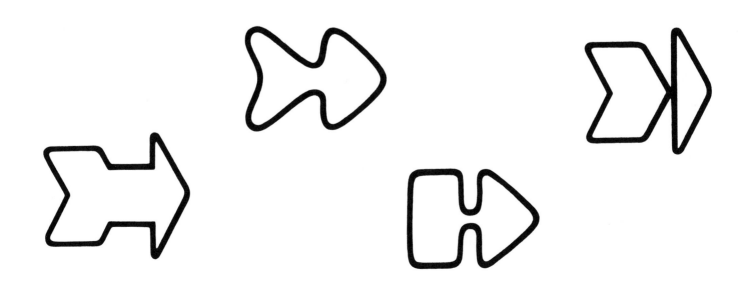

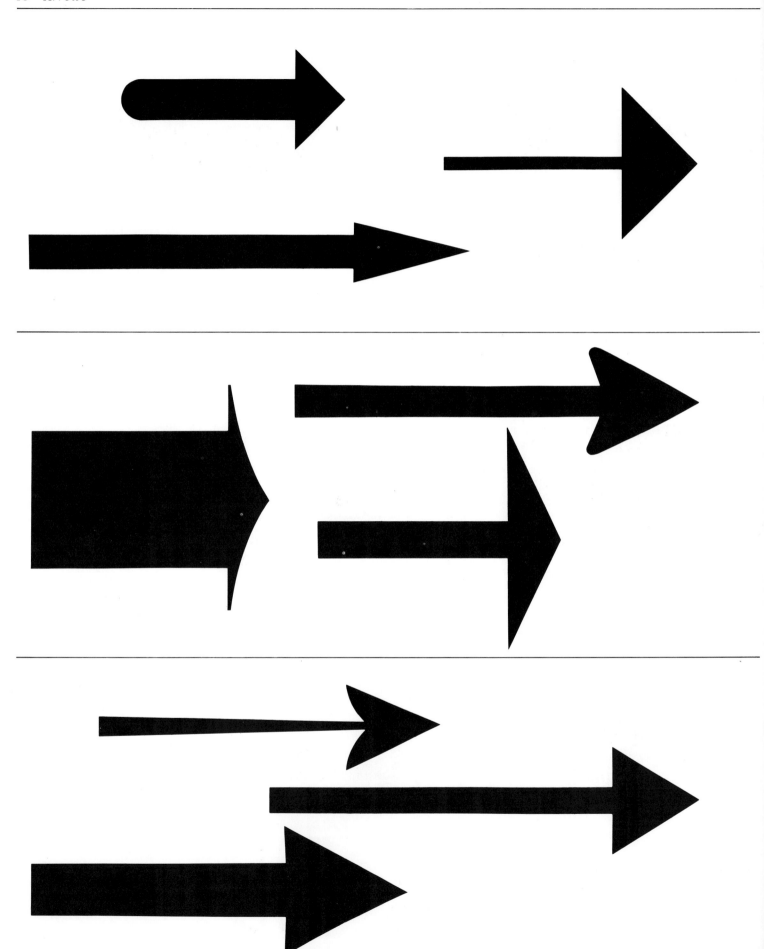

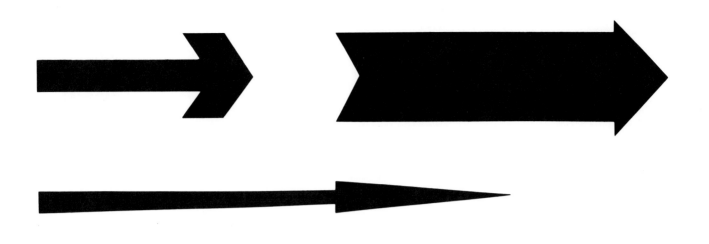

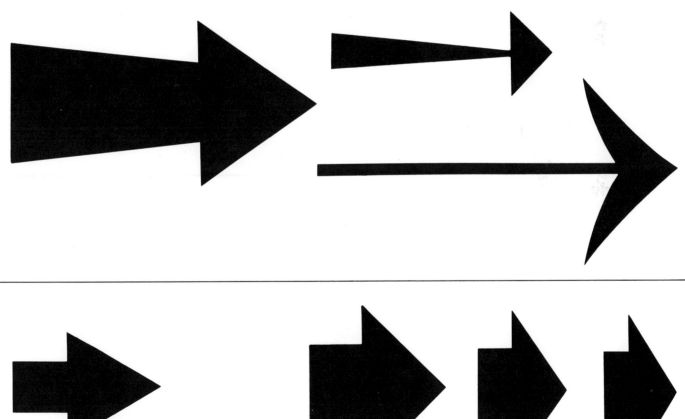

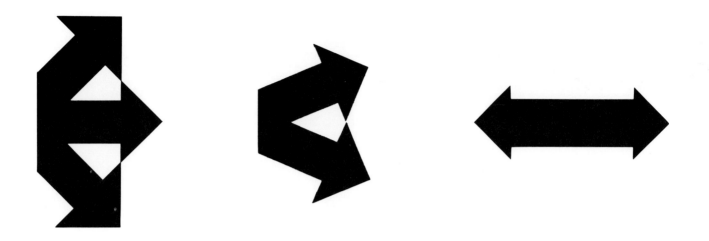

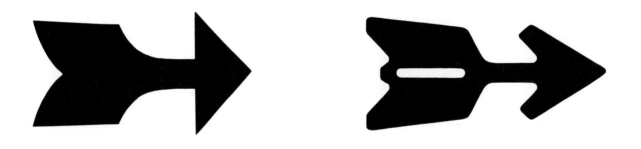

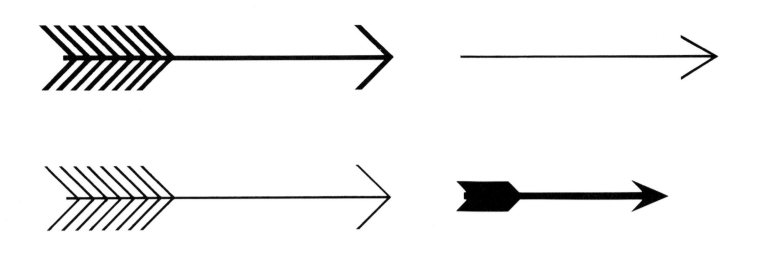

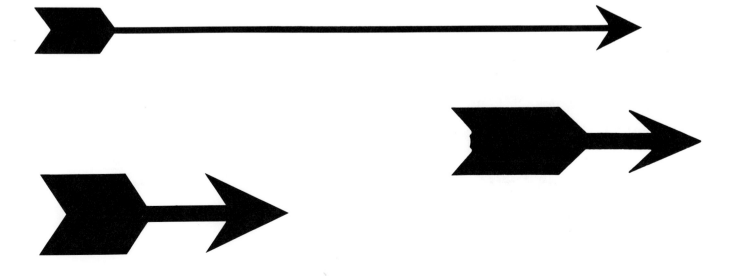

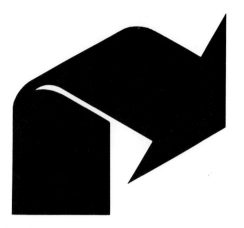

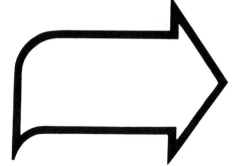
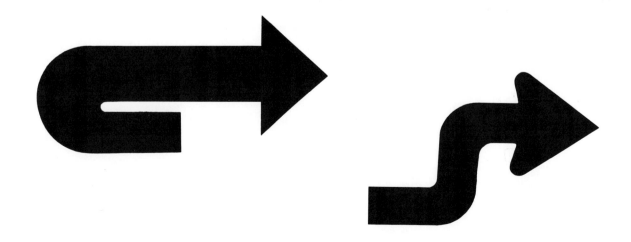

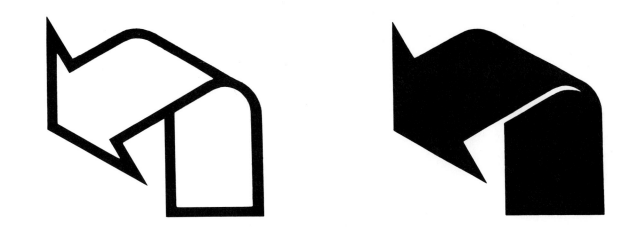

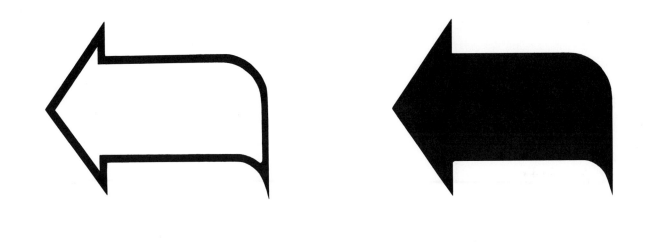

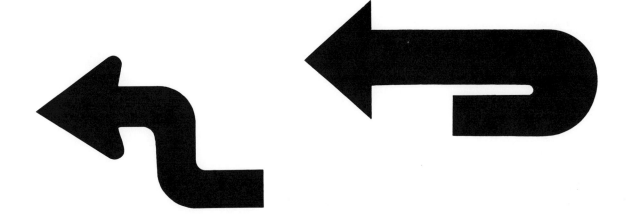

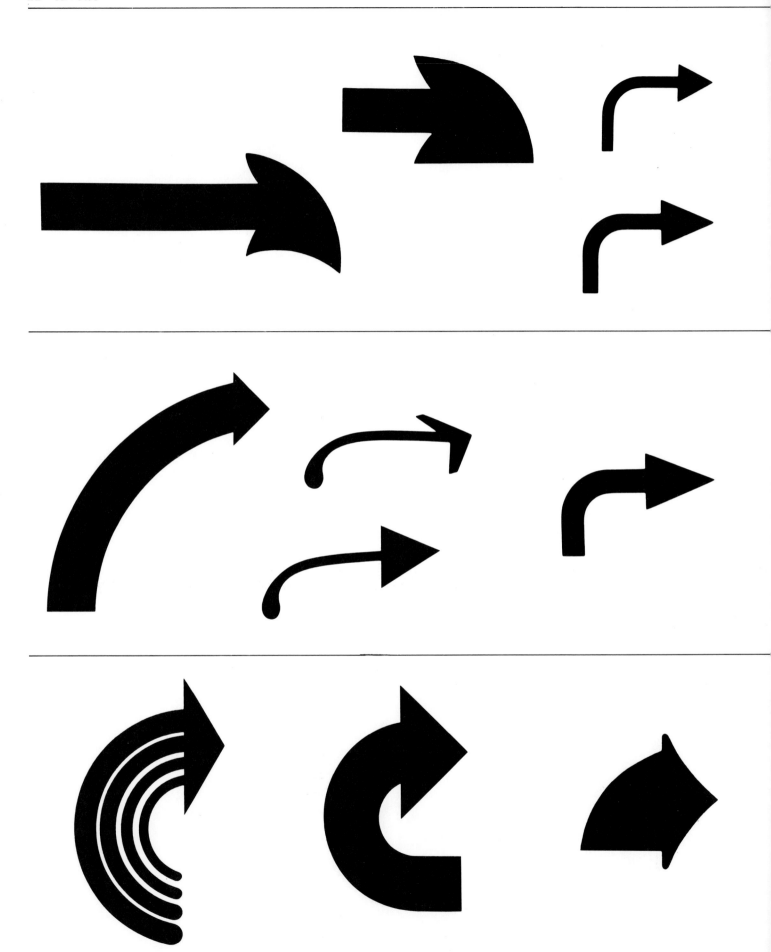

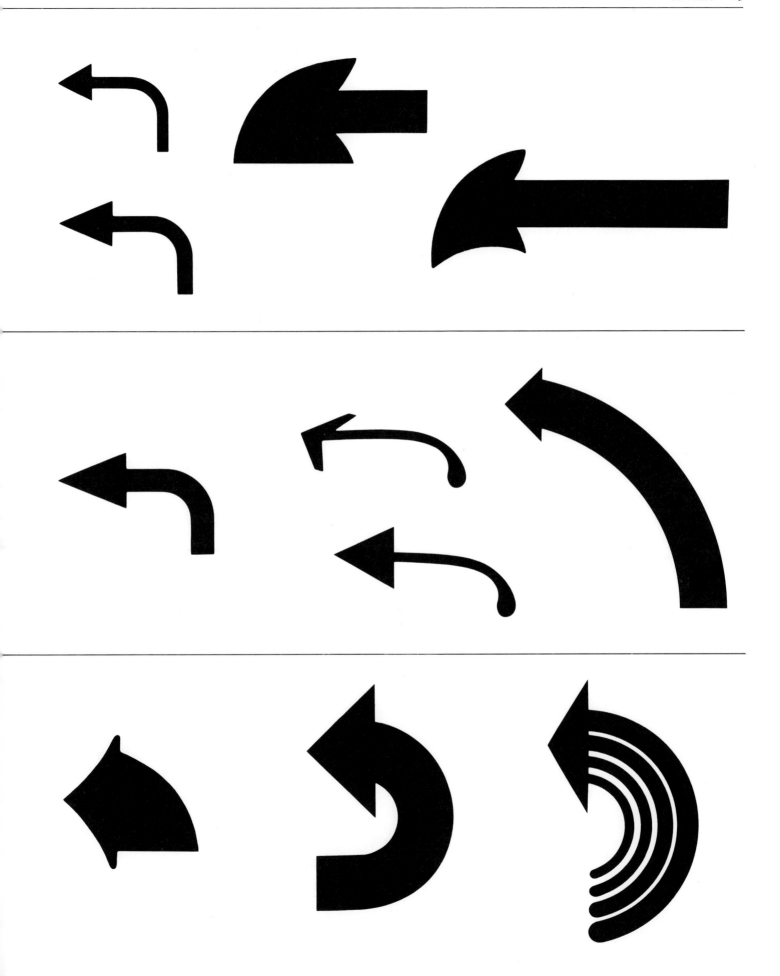

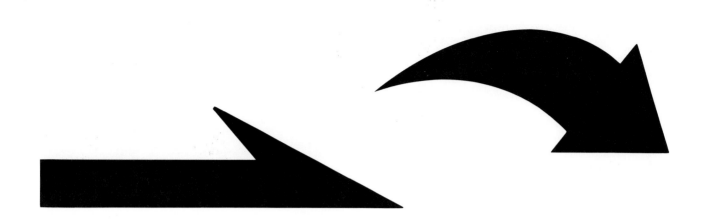

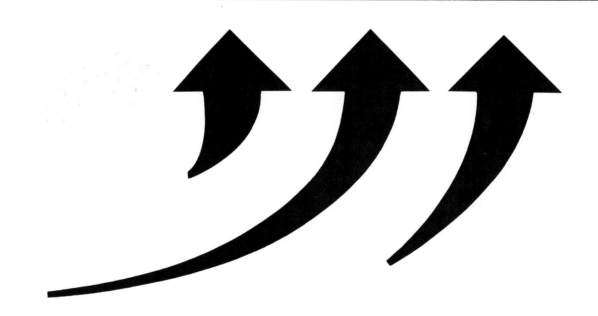

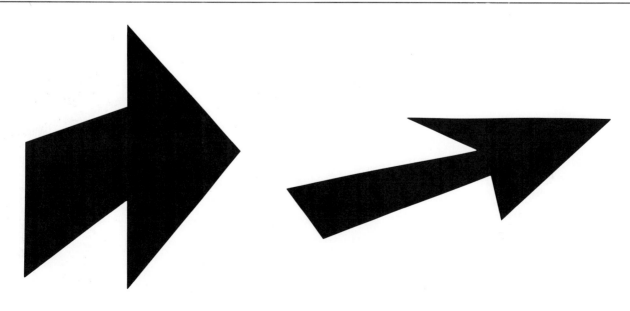

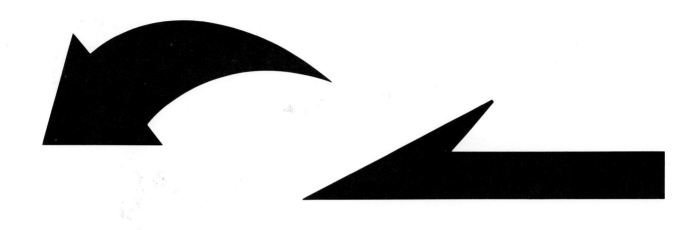

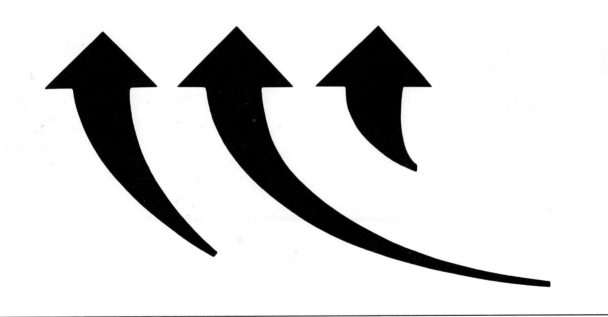

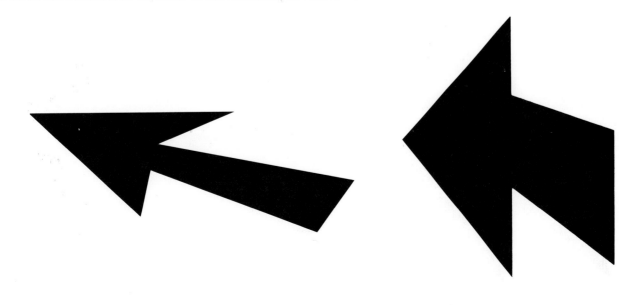

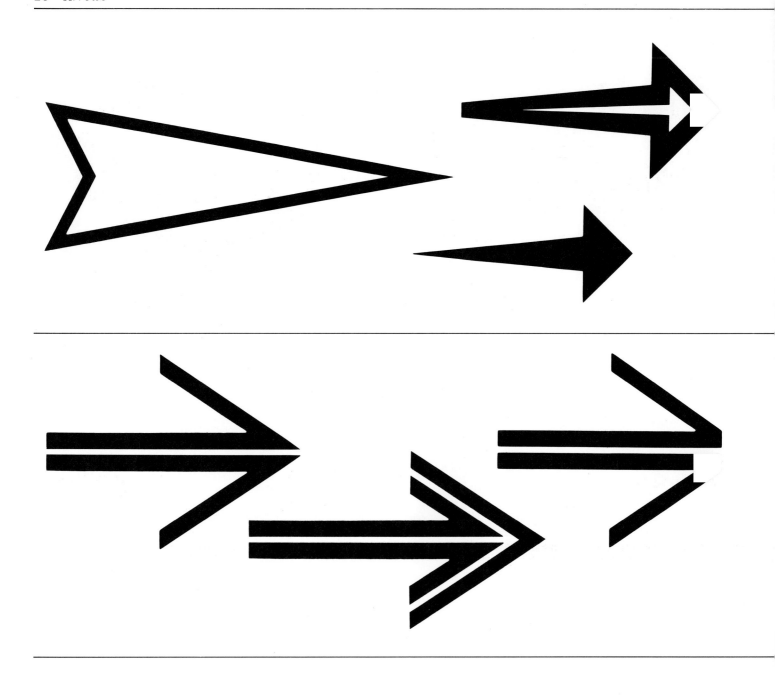

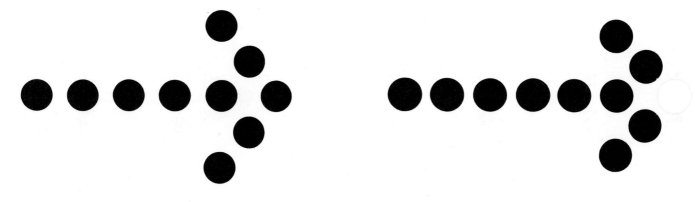

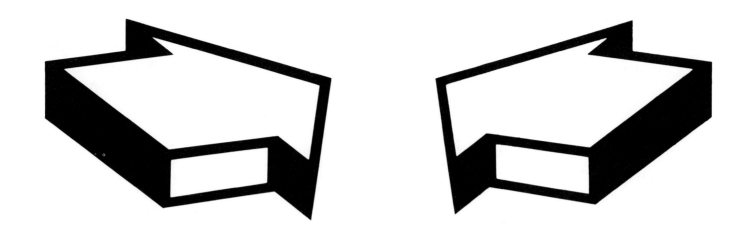

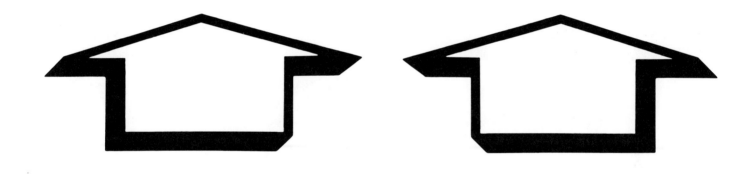

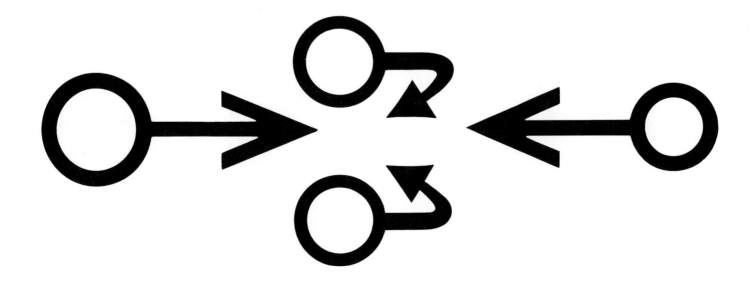

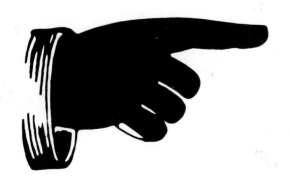

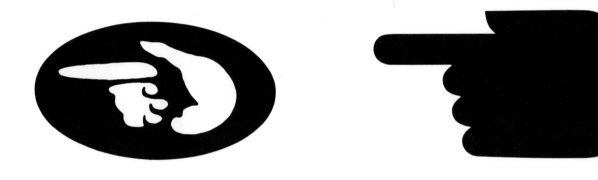

Seals
Labels
Postage Motifs
Tags
Blurbs
Bursts
Banners

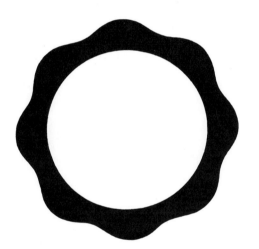

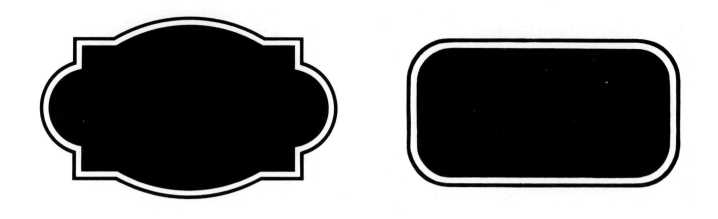

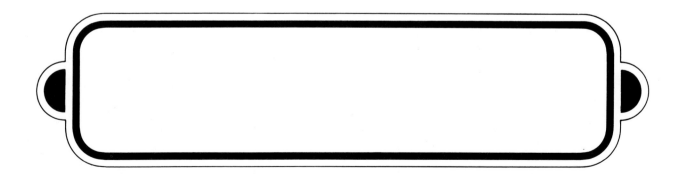

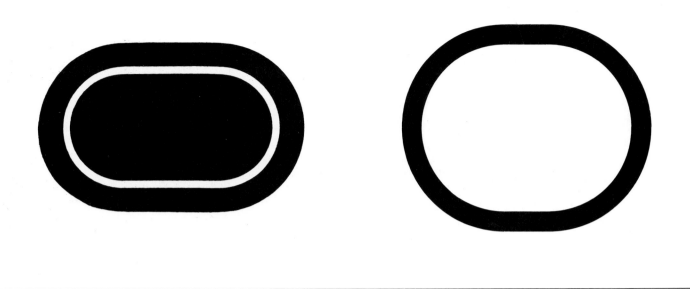

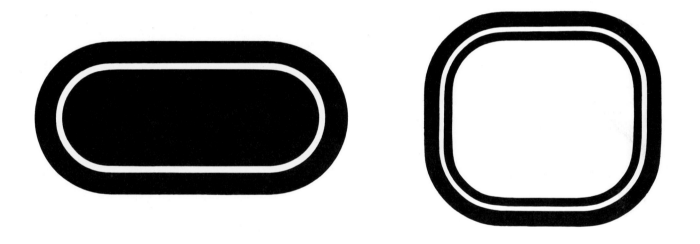

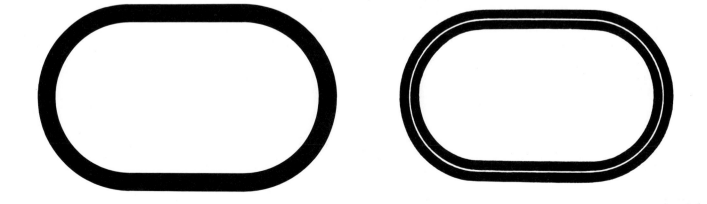

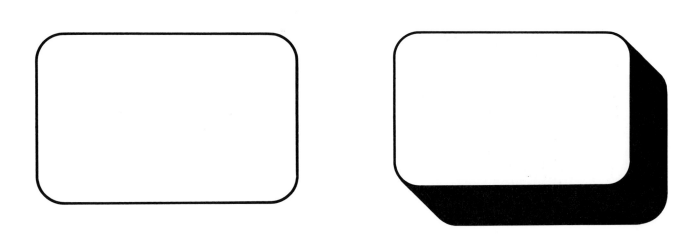

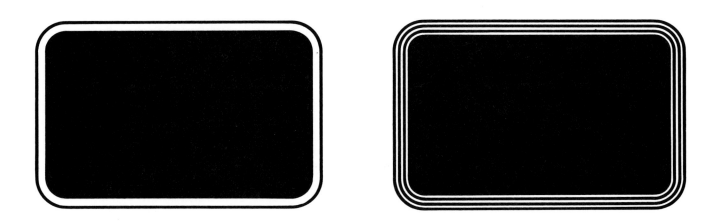

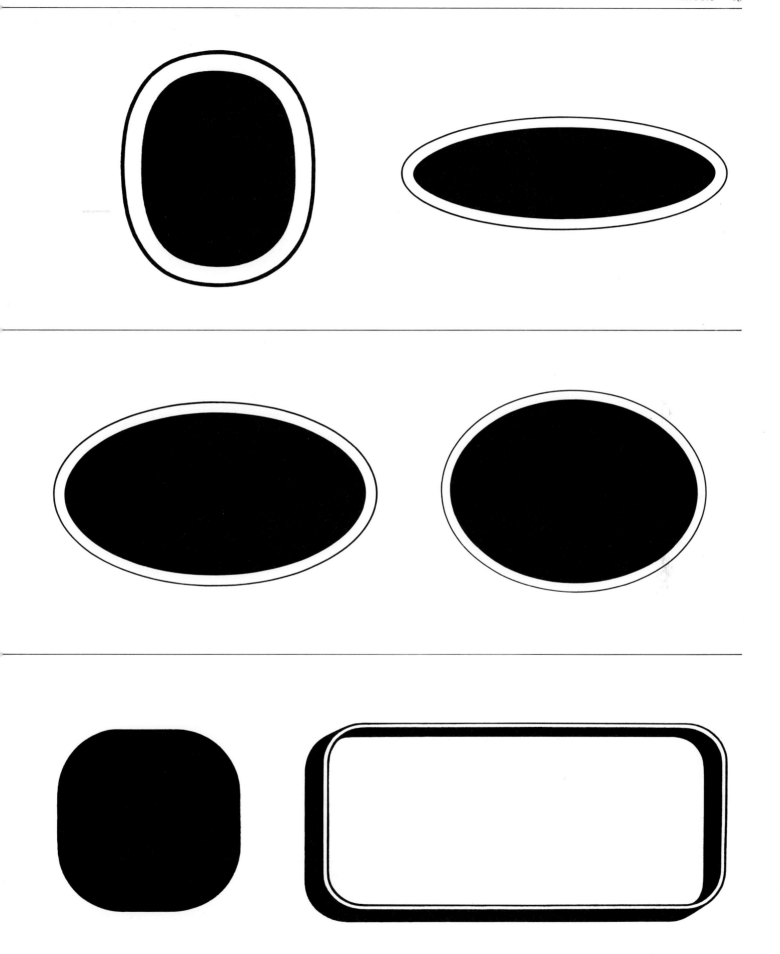

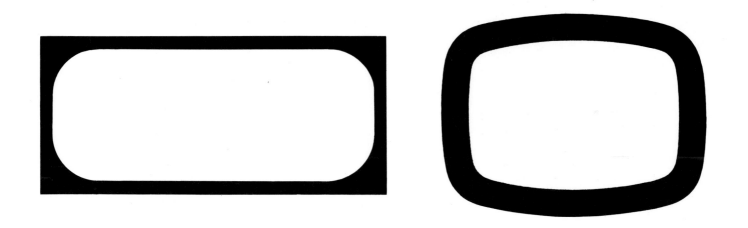

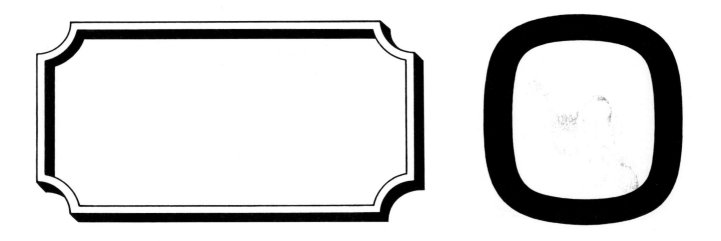

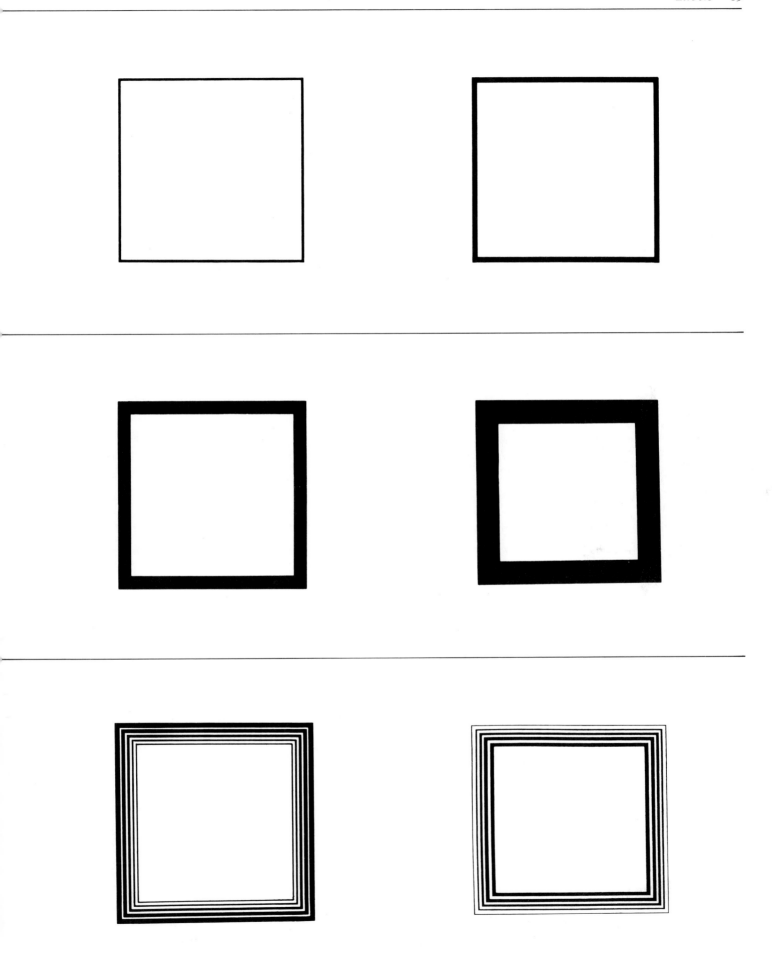

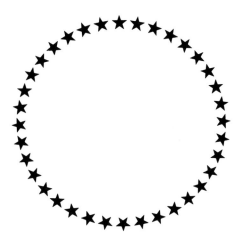
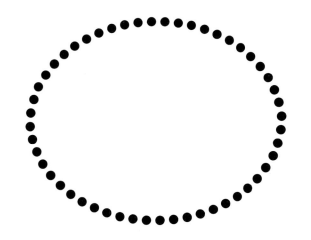
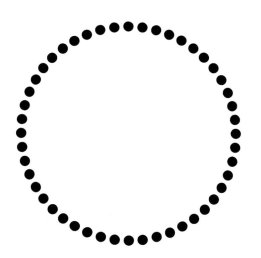

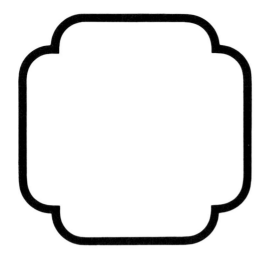

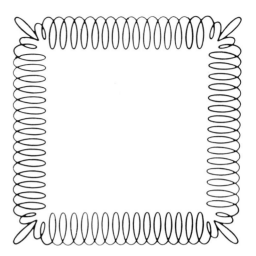

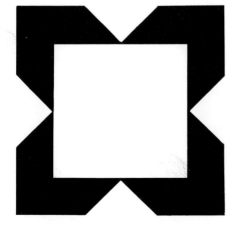

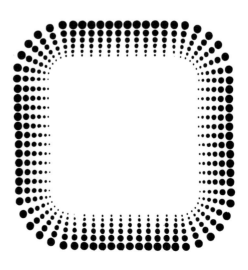

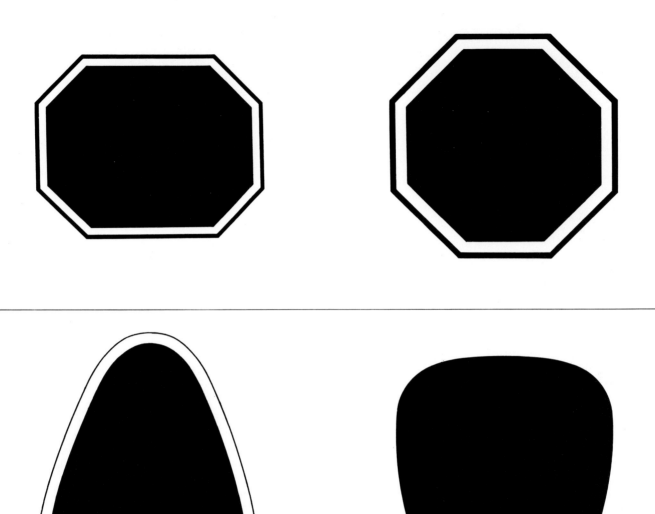

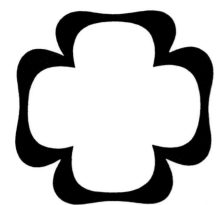

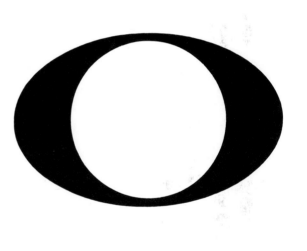
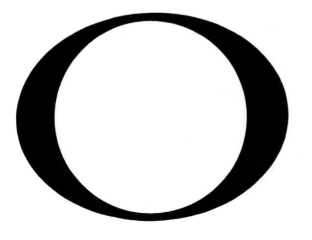
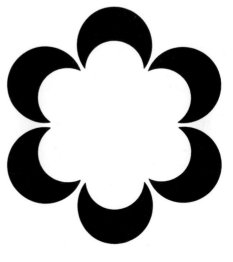

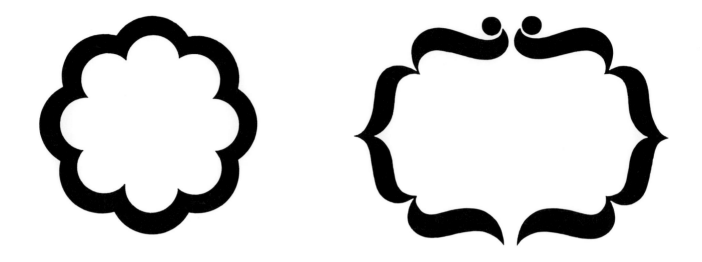

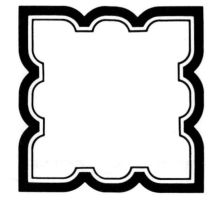

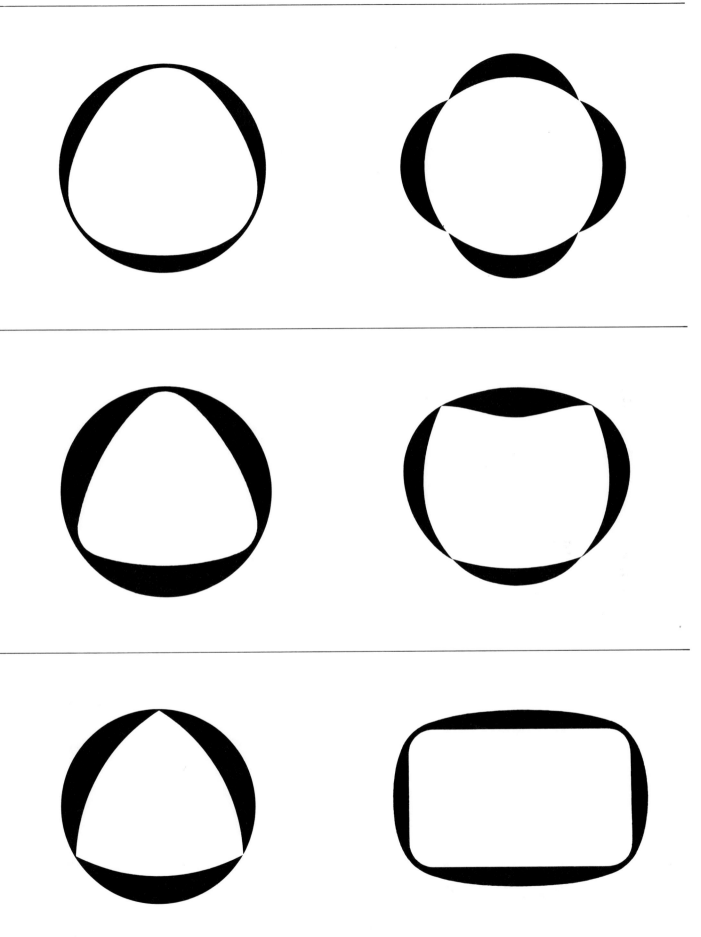

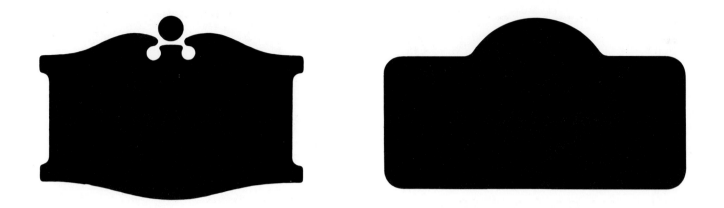

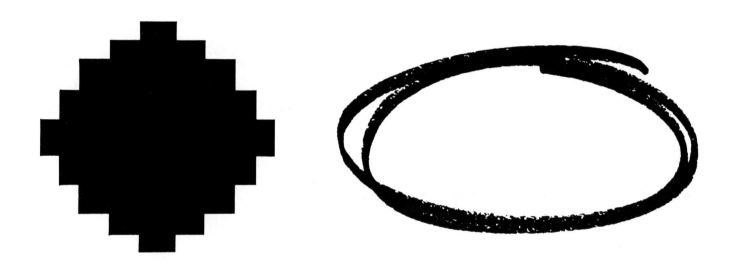

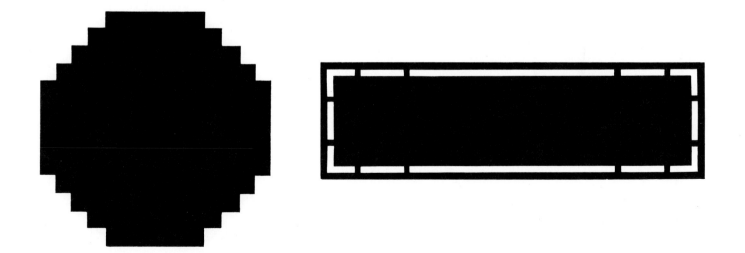

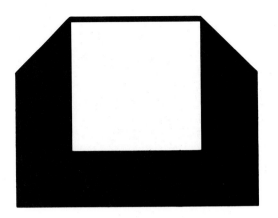

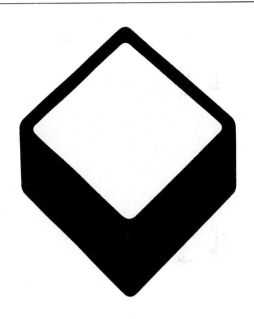

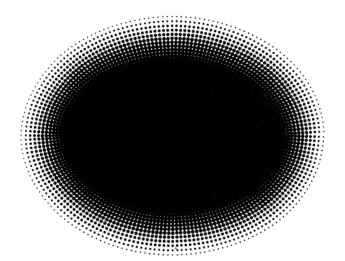

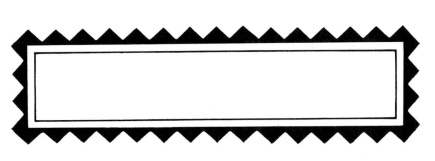

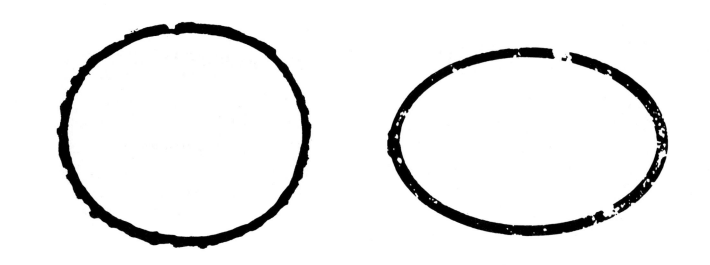

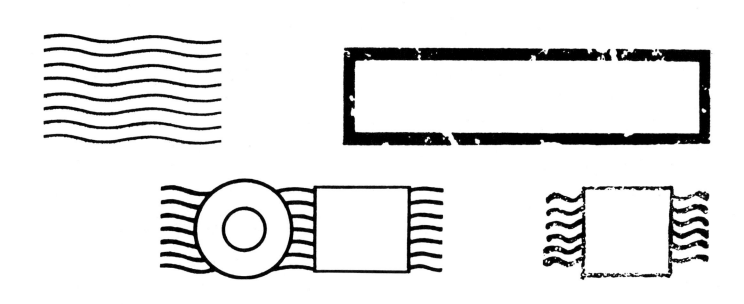

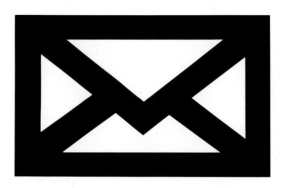

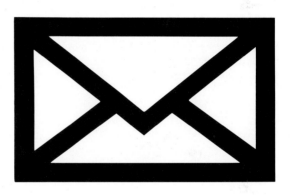

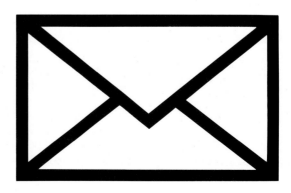

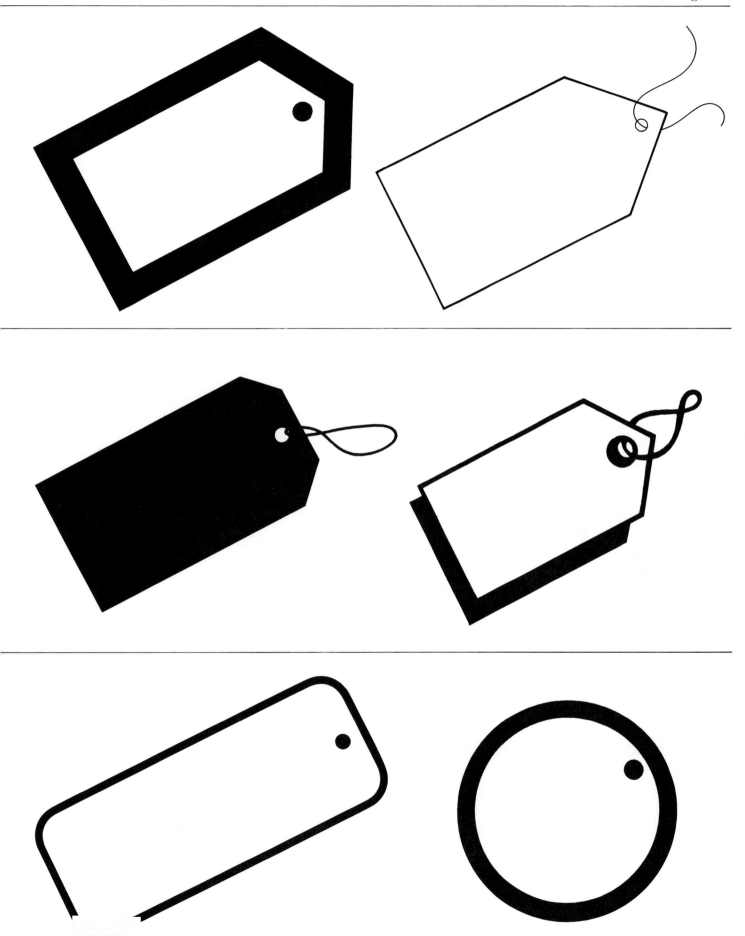

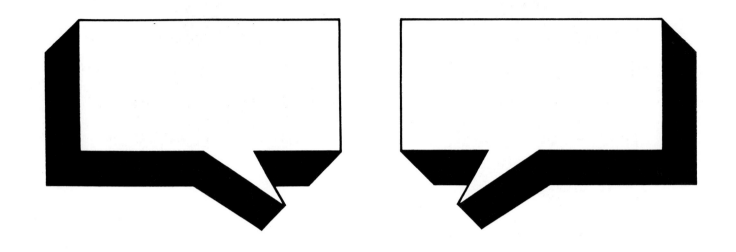

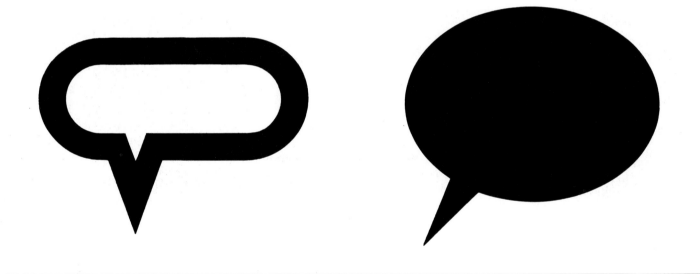

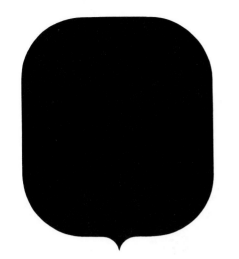

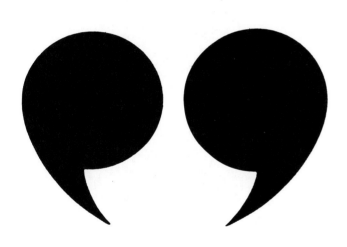

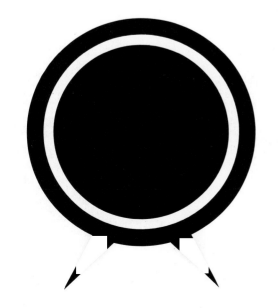

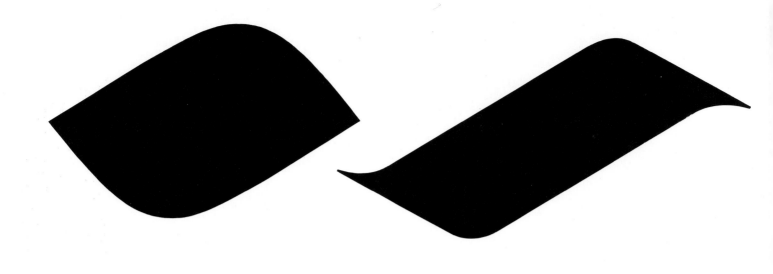

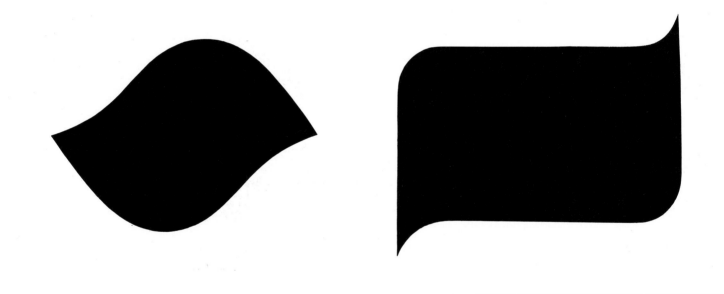

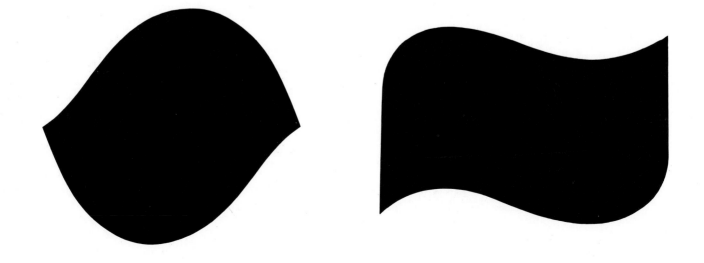

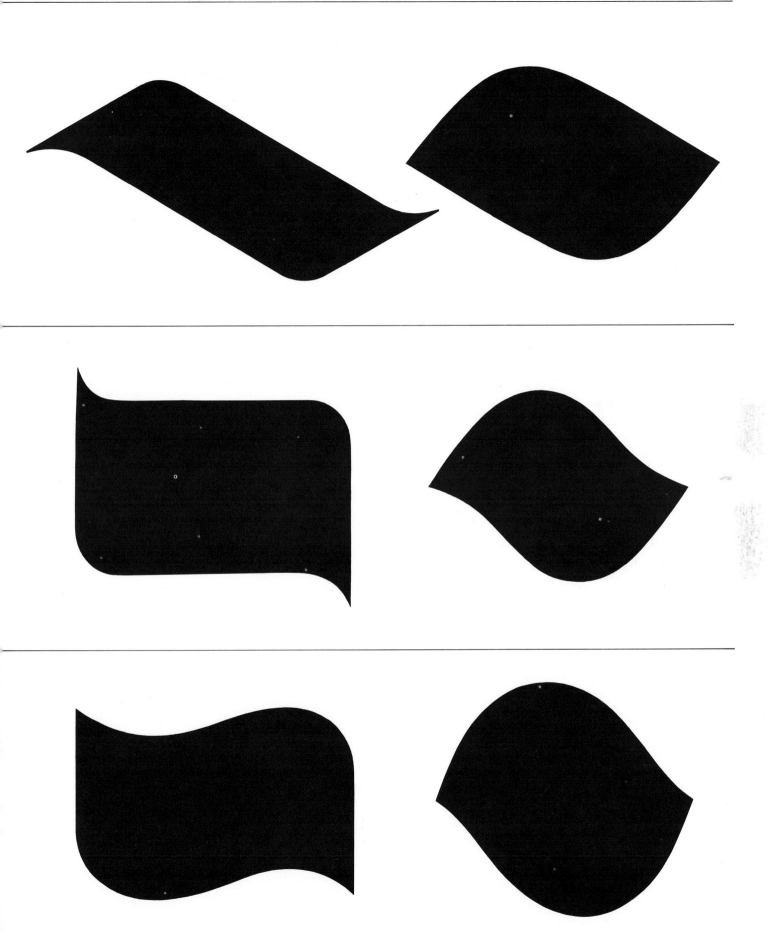

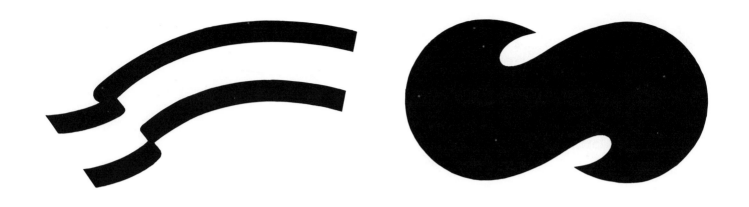

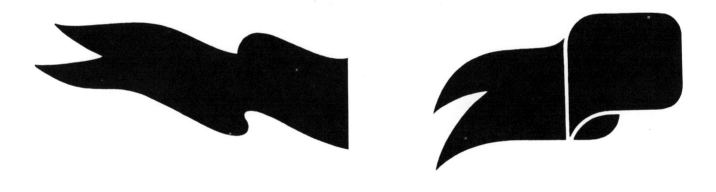

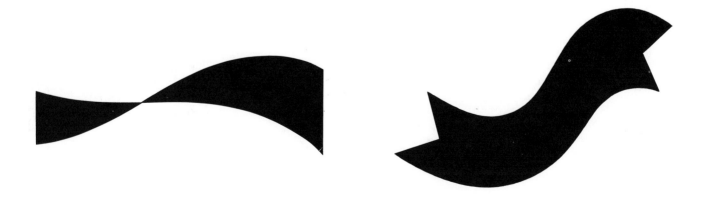

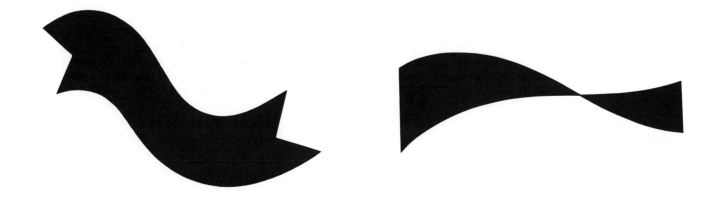

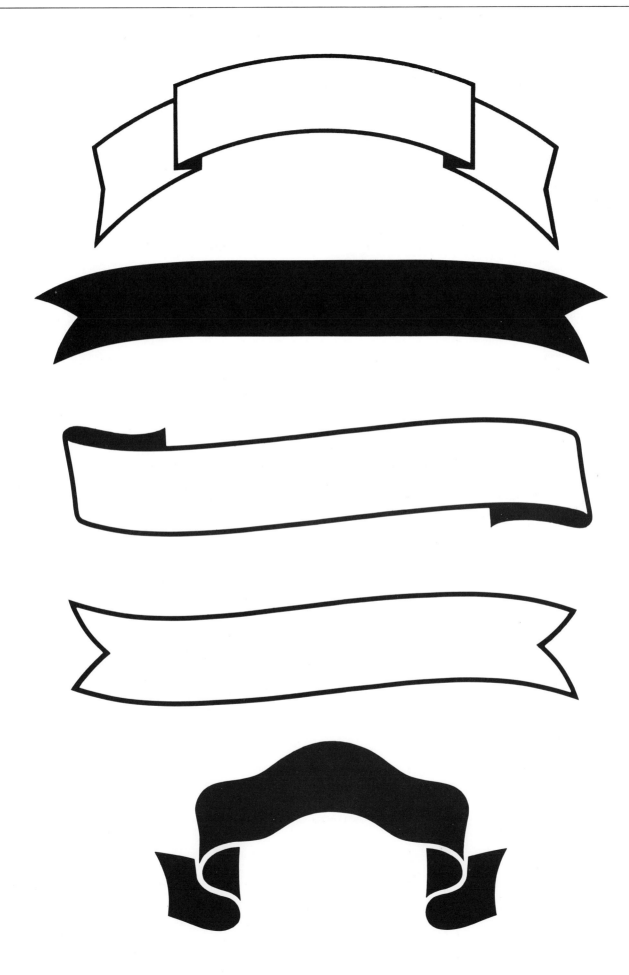

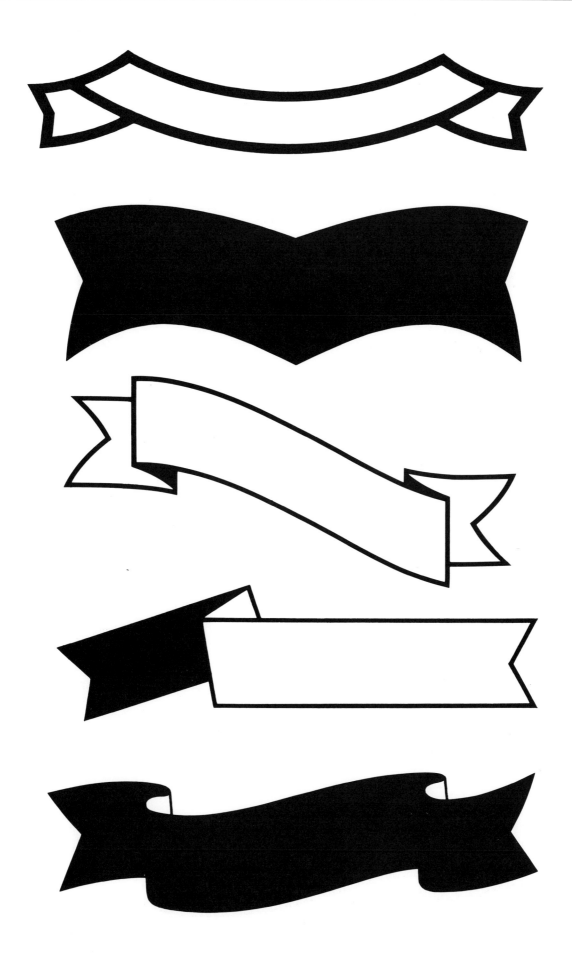

Hearts
Playing Card Symbols
Lips
Leaf Shapes
Trees
Crowns/Coronets
Flame Shapes
Clouds
Teardrops
Light Bulb Shapes
Eggs
Pear Shapes, etc.
Bell Shapes

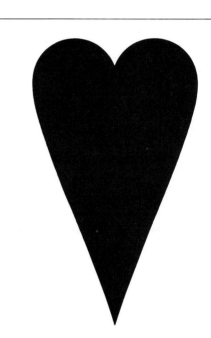

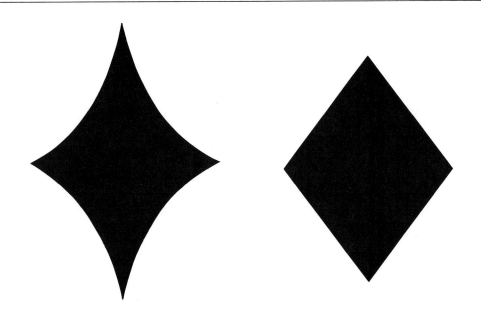

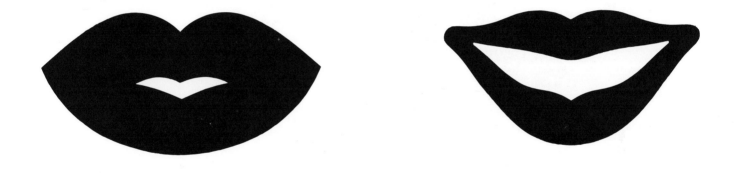

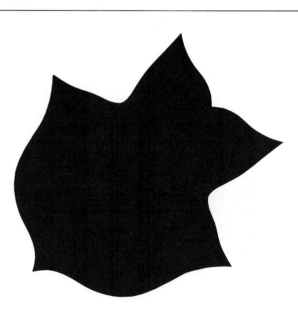

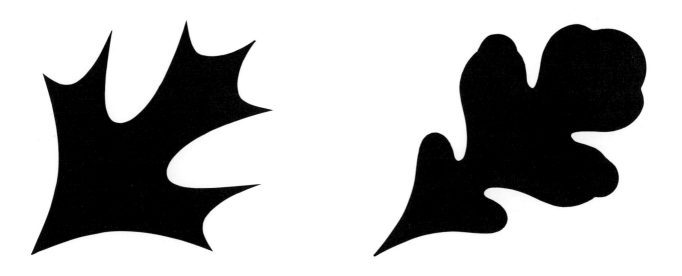

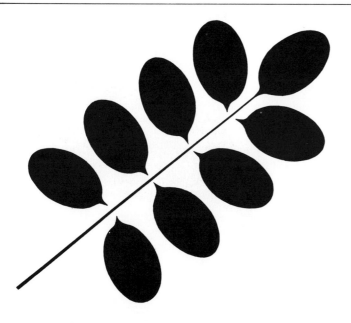

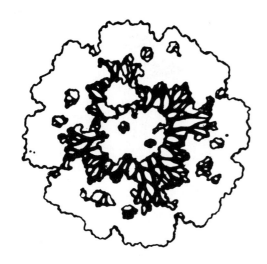

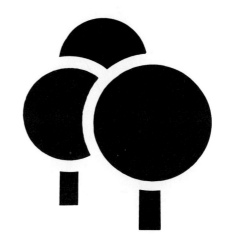

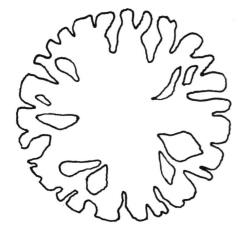

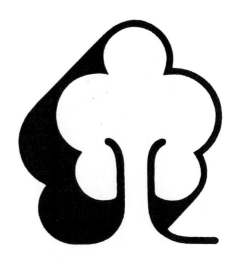

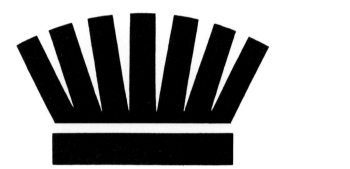

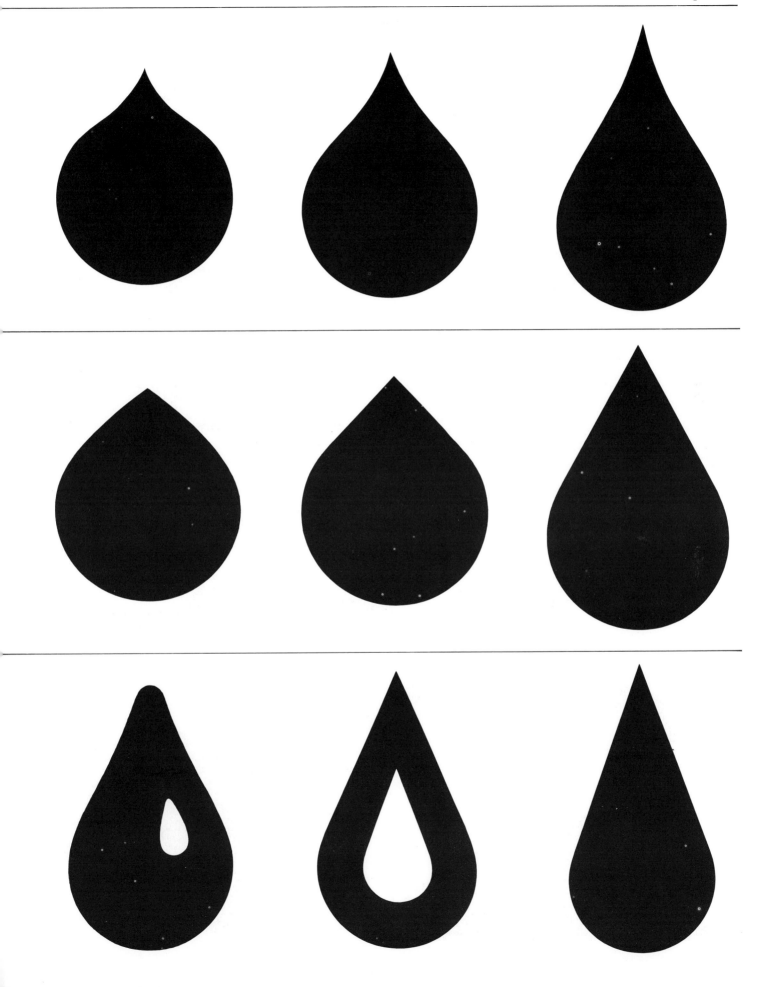

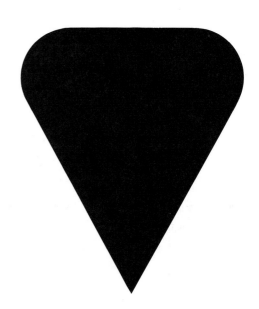

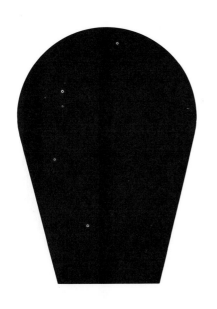

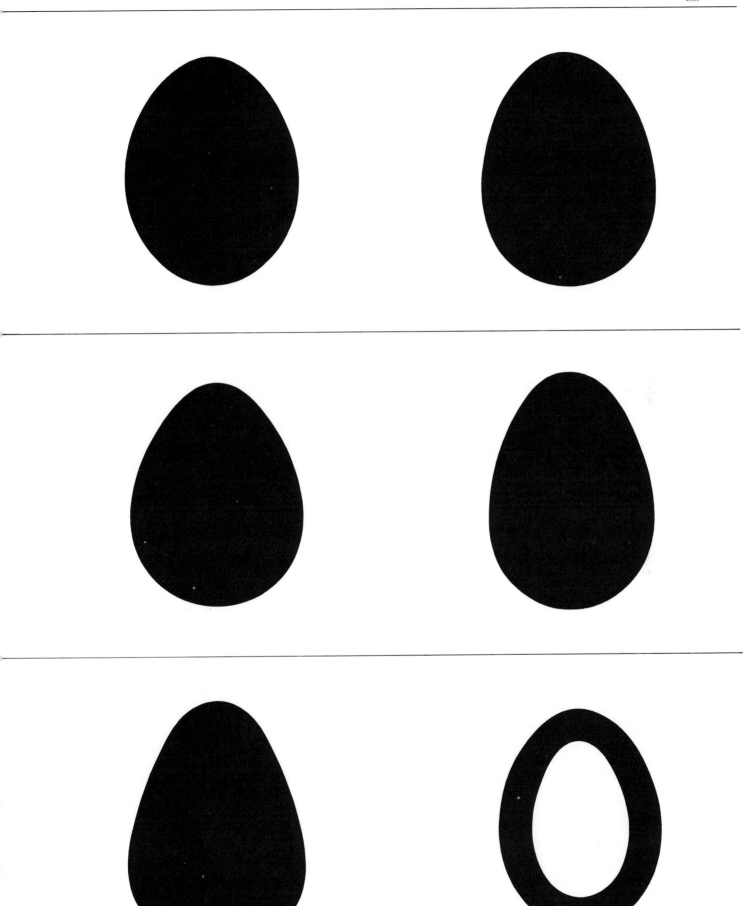

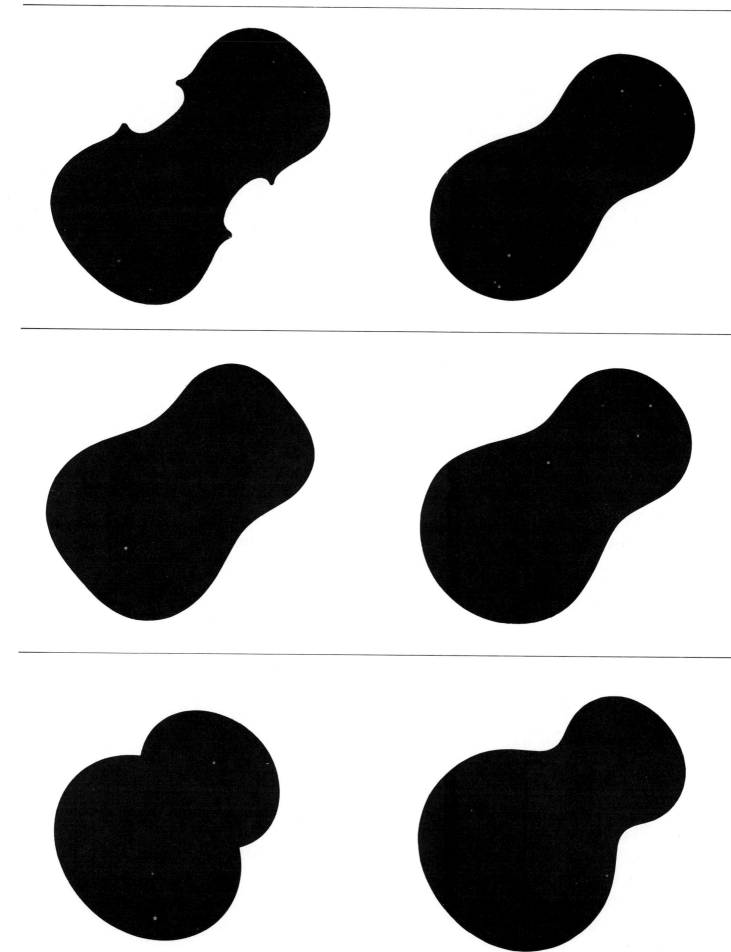

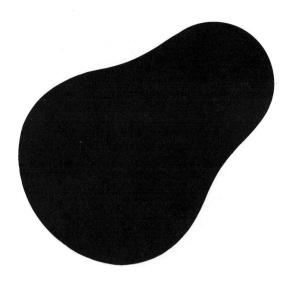

*General
Design Elements
including:
Film Strips
Arches/Parabolas
Boomerangs
Magnets
Diamond Shapes
Pentagons
Springs/Coils
Cross Shapes
Yin Yang Symbols
Atomic Symbols
Keyholes
Palettes
Hour Glasses
Infinity Symbols
Dart Boards
Globes*

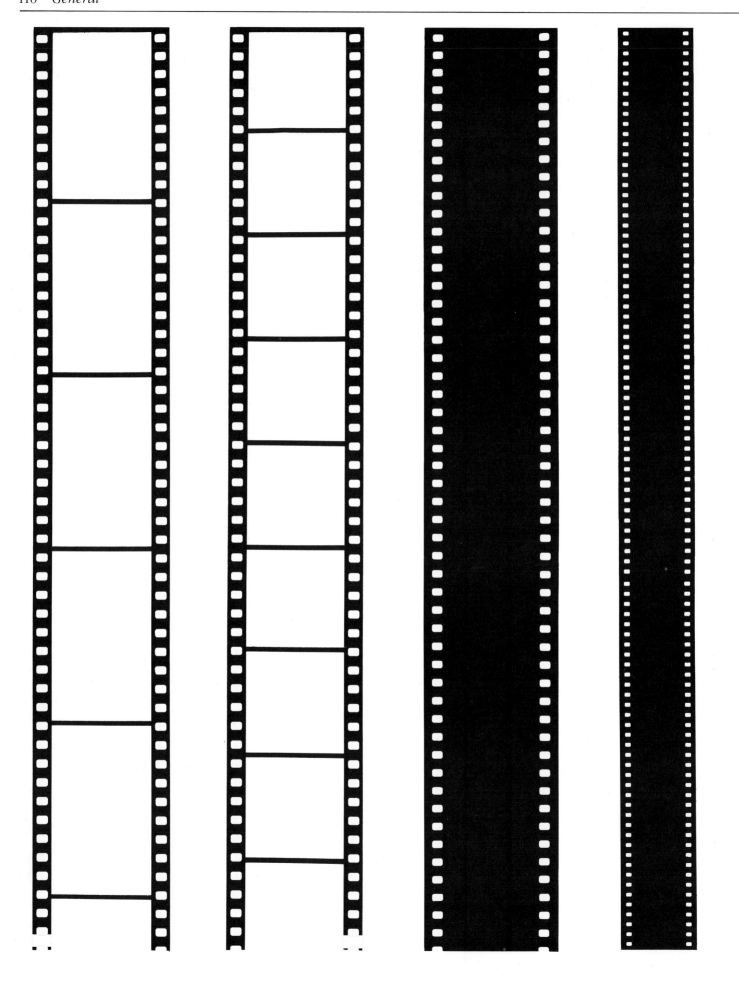

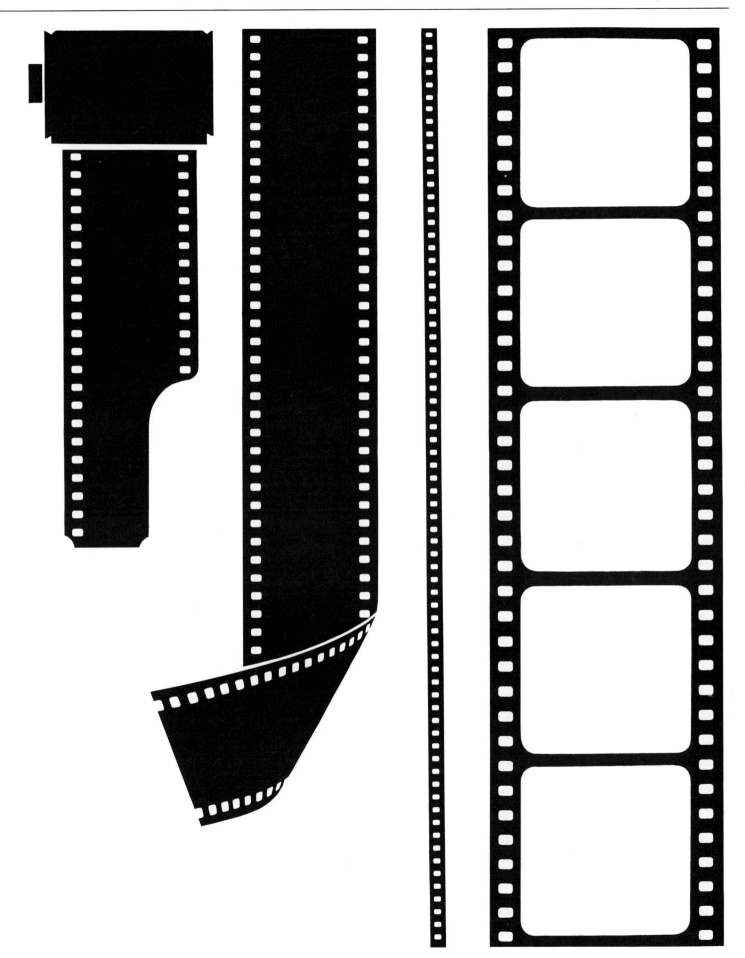

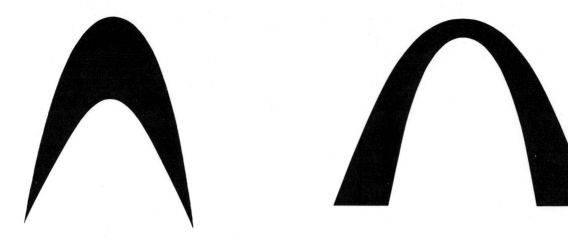

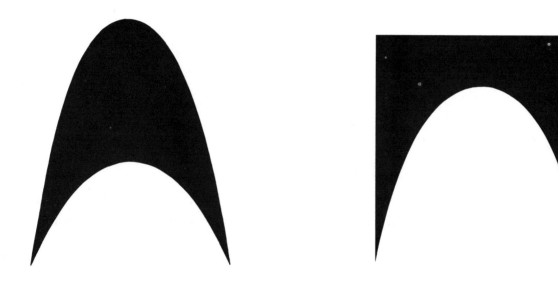

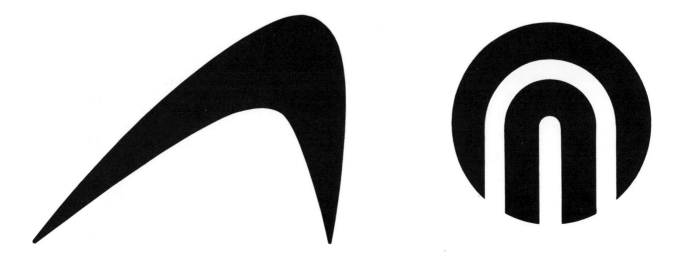

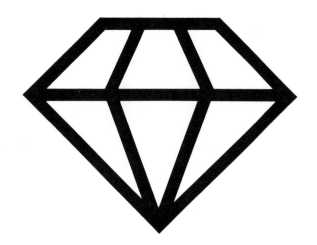

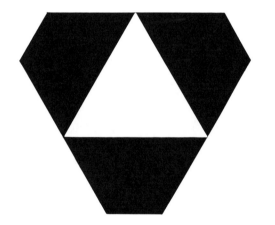
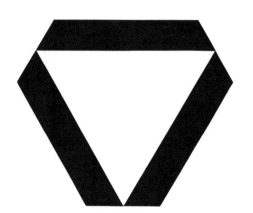

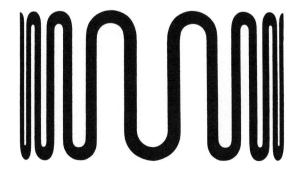

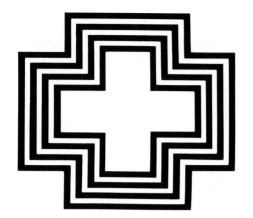

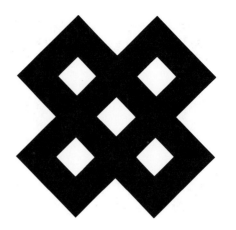

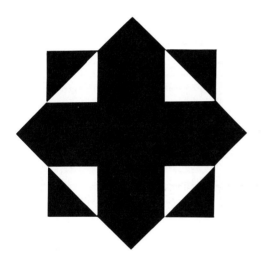

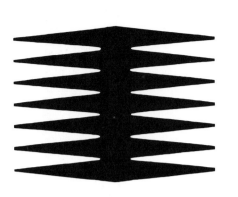

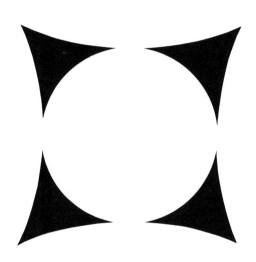

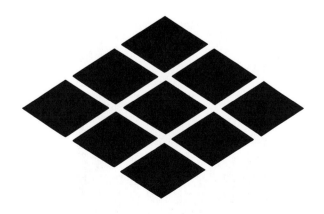

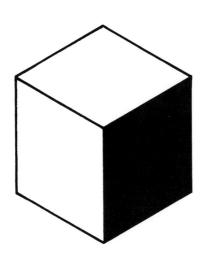
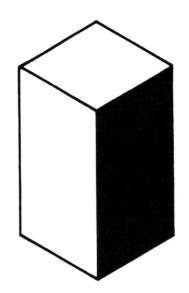

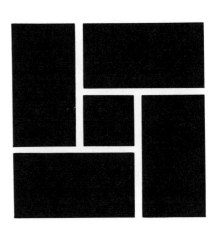

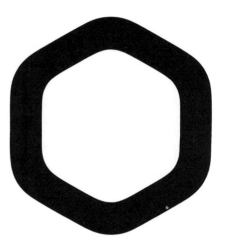

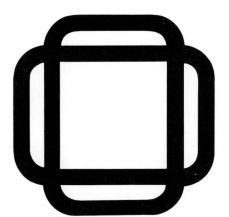

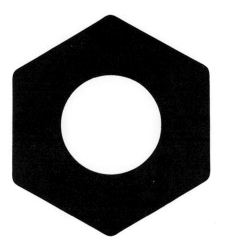

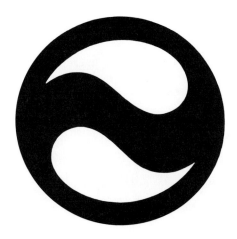

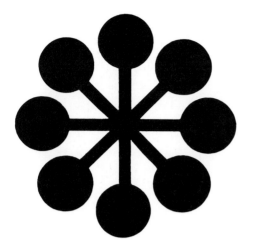

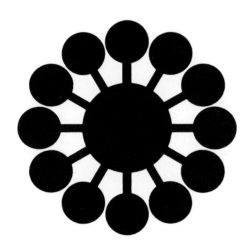

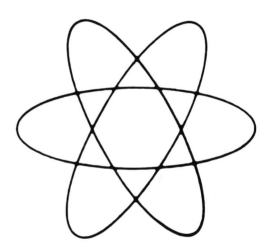

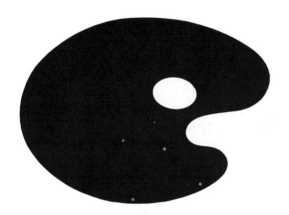
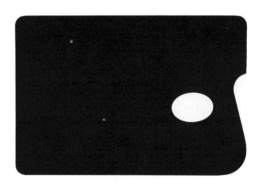

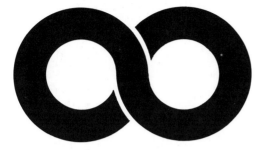

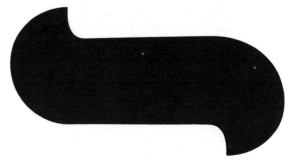

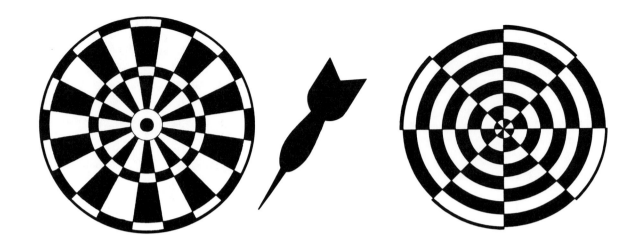